Today's Donkey in the "New World"

Donkeys of the Caribbean

Photography and Narration by Mark S. Meyers

Published, Photographed and Narrated by
Mark S. Meyers
3524 Knickerbocker Road C-340
San Angelo, TX 76904
theburroman@gmail.com

For information on the work of the Peaceful Valley Donkey Rescue
PO Box 216
Miles, TX 76861
866-366-5731
info@pvdr.org
www.donkeyrescue.org

ISBN #978-0-9771471-5-1

For Amy, the love of my life, for always believing in me.
Thank you for 25 great years.

Preface

When I finished Talking With Donkeys 4, I dropped the mike and walked off stage. I figured I had written my last book. It wasn't a negative thing, I just knew I had run out of things to write about. TWD 1-4 were based on me, my family, my rescue and I felt I had adequately covered the subject. It wasn't until we had to order an additional 1,500 copies that I started missing the writing process.

The premise for this book came from an invitation to speak at the 2017 Donkey Welfare Symposium in Davis California in the Fall. I had been asked to speak on Donkey Basketball, Donkey Races and Donkey Roping. As I wrapped my mind around how I wanted to approach the subject, a thought came to me; I could approach the project as Mark the Donkey Rescuer or I could approach it as an outside party simply reporting on the situation.

As a rescuer I would be predisposed to be anti-everything that I found because it didn't fit my particular belief system. The reality is these activities are part of the current state of donkeys, regardless of how I feel about it, it is happening. So I took one big step backwards and thought about all of the other things donkeys are doing throughout the US, both good and bad. One more step back and I was thinking about all of the donkeys in the Americas.

Donkeys arrived in the New World with Christopher Columbus on his second voyage which put them in the Americas sometime in late 1493. So I thought, maybe a book about the current state of donkeys throughout all of the Americas. The more research I did, the more excited I became. Then a cold realization hit me… I could write about the Caribbean and North America easily enough but I would totally have to "phone in" Central and South America or let the project linger for the next several years as I established contacts in these regions.

So… new plan. This is the first in what I hope is a three book series. I started with the Caribbean because that is where the donkeys first came to the Americas, so it kind of felt right. Amy, as always, was supportive of the concept and made it easy for me to take off for two weeks so that I could photograph and interview for this book.

Once again, I am NOT a writer. If it is fancy words you are seeking, put this one down and grab yourself another. I am not a passionate person unless we are talking about my beautiful wife or my work with donkeys. I hope that passion shines through my lack of writing skills and you can get a clear understanding of the Donkeys of the Caribbean.

MSM

Introduction

In 1493, Christopher Columbus brought horses, cattle, goats and donkeys to the island of Hispaniola (we call it the Dominican Republic and Haiti). As more and more islands were settled by Europeans, agriculture and mining increased and so did the need for donkeys. Donkeys were traded between islands and imported from Europe until there were donkeys on almost every island in the Caribbean.

I chose three islands for the basis for this book; Bonaire, Sint. Eustatius (Statia) and Nevis. I could have chosen several others but I felt these three represented all of the problems/situations that donkeys face in the Caribbean and I already had established connections to all three islands. I spent two weeks among the Caribbean Donkeys and I will share with you, as accurately as I can, my experiences.

Many of the people that support my work with the donkeys in the United States have expressed their reluctance to support my efforts in the Caribbean. They feel that since there are so many issues that we are dealing with in the states, why do we need to take on other country's problems as well? To me, the answer is simple, either all donkeys matter or none of them do. When I see a donkey in need, I have to try and help it. It is simply who I am.

Unlike Will Rogers, I have met many men who I do not like, but for almost 20 years, I have never met a donkey that I didn't like and respect. Maybe by the time you finish this book, you will join me in trying to help the Donkeys of the Caribbean.

Bonaire

Country: Netherlands (Special Municipality)

Capital: Kralendijk

Area: 114 square miles

Human Population: 19,905

Donkey Population: >1,000

Florida

THE BAHAMAS

NASSAU

HAVANA

CUBA

Cayman Islands

GEORGE TOWN

Guantanamo Bay

HAITI

PORT-AU-PRINCE

KINGSTON

SANTO DOMINGO

DOMINICAN REPUBLIC

San Juan
SAN JUAN

British Virgin Islands

PUERTO RICO

Virgin Islands

ROAD TOWN

CHARLOTTE AMALIE

Anguilla
THE VALLEY

ANTIGUA & BARBUDA

BASSETERRE

SAINT KITTS & NEVIS

ST. JOHN'S

Montserrat

Guadeloupe
BASSE-TERRE

DOMINICA
ROSEAU

Martinique
FORT-DE-FRANCE

CASTRIES
SAINT LUCIA

BARBADOS

KINGSTOWN
BRIDGETOWN

SAINT VINCENT & THE GRENADINES

GRENADA
ST. GEORGE'S

CARIBBEAN SEA

Aruba
ORANJESTAD

Netherlands Antilles

WILLEMSTAD

PORT-OF-SPAIN

TRINIDAD & TOBAGO

CARACAS

RICA

COLOMBIA

PANAMA
PANAMA

VENEZUELA

When imagining the Caribbean, most people do not think "donkeys". Beautiful beaches, clear oceans, all inclusive resorts… but not donkeys. Many therefore are surprised to learn that not only are there donkeys on many Caribbean islands, but they are in peril on some of them. Animals in general do not fare well on the islands. Dog overpopulation is rampant and on one particular island there are tens of thousands of monkeys, none of these animals are indigenous and many are out of control.

Peaceful Valley first got involved in the Caribbean because of social media. There I was minding my own business, fixing the donkey problems of the United States when I received a phone call. The lady on the other end of the phone asked if I could intervene on behalf of the Donkey Sanctuary on Bonaire. A person from the United States had taken a tour of the sanctuary and wrote a scathing critique on her blog. As a result, the sanctuary was losing donations and was under constant attack on their Facebook page.

In all honesty, I was not completely unbiased in my approach to this problem. These same people had tried to attack Peaceful Valley in the past and I knew, for a fact, that they never let the truth get in the way of their agenda. Their attempts at PVDR failed but they were gaining ground on Bonaire. But…I am not in this business to counter false claims against fellow rescuers, I am in this business to help donkeys. So with that in mind, Amy and I packed up our bikinis, swim fins and video cameras and headed off to Bonaire.

Bonaire is a fantastic place to visit. It offers beach and boat scuba diving, snorkeling, kite surfing and wind surfing not to mention great restaurants, casinos and of course, donkeys. English is the everyday language and they conveniently use the American dollar. I have visited the island twice and both times stayed at the Divi Flamingo. A little historical sidetrack; The Airport was originally built as a military airstrip for service in World War II and the Divi Flamingo was originally a prisoner of war camp for German and Dutch Nazis. Since history is critical to understanding the plight of the Caribbean Donkey, y'all are going to be learning a little something along the way too.

Bonaire, along with Aruba and Curacao, are often referred to as the ABC islands and were originally named 'las Islas de los Gigantes' or 'the islands of the giants" by the Spaniards because of the tall indigenous people. The Spaniards saw little use for the islands and removed all of the natives to work the mines on Hispaniola. In 1526, cattle, goats and donkeys were imported from Spain and Bonaire was set up as a plantation. Later under Dutch rule, the salt pans were mined and worked by slaves and donkeys alike. The slave huts still stand along the beach and a colored spire sits near each group of huts. These spires were a signal to ships and indicated the grade of salt that was available at each encampment. As modern machinery became available the donkeys were eventually phased out and forgotten about.

When Amy and I took our first trip to the island, we divided the task at hand. She was going to inspect and report on the conditions on the sanctuary and I was going to assess the condition of the donkeys and range outside of the sanctuary. We also interviewed the staff, tourists, government officials and locals to try and get a feel for what was really going on. We tried to get an interview with the people on the island that stood in opposition to the Sanctuary, but they ignored our requests until we returned to the United States, at which time they disputed ever receiving our requests but yet they somehow knew we made the requests in order to dispute ever receiving them…it is all very confusing but I think I can true it up as we continue our Bonairian Journey.

Basically what we found was that the donkeys on the sanctuary were thriving. They had plenty to eat, quality medical care and an attentive staff. The sanctuary is built along the premise of tourism, so people can actually drive through and get up close and personal with the donkeys

The donkeys are fed twice per day; in the morning they receive a pelleted feed and in the evening they are given donated produce and grass hay. Tourism is a major part of the sanctuary's finances and when the attacks began, the tour bus drivers and others shied away and therefore the sanctuary suffered as a result.

The donkeys living outside the sanctuary were not faring as well. The Caribbean had been in a drought and there was very little forage. The donkeys looked thin and were forced to encroach more and more on the human areas of the island. The donkeys were getting into trash bins, crossing busy roads and finding their way into the dump. Donkey related traffic accidents were on the rise and many of the times, the donkeys were killed. In my opinion I felt the island could only host 200 free roaming donkeys. This meant that the Sanctuary's plan of bringing in the females and babies and castrating and rereleasing the males was a sound approach to solving the overpopulation problem.

Amy and I were in full agreement that the claims made by the opposition group were completely false. None of their claims were true and they were motivated by their philosophy that donkeys, all donkeys, should be left to their own devices and not managed. This not only includes these tiny Caribbean Islands, but also in the United States. In my opinion, and I have been associated with donkeys, both wild and domestic, for going on 20 years, this is ridiculous. Donkeys are feral animals with no real predation to control their numbers, therefore they will continue to breed and overpopulate and then suffer when droughts or other factors limit their food sources. Amy and I made a film based on our findings and hopefully made a difference to the Sanctuary. You can watch "The Donkeys of Bonaire" on our Youtube channel at www.donkeyrescue.tv

Marina Melis and I became good friends during this investigation. She is the founder of Donkey Sanctuary Bonaire and is a kindred spirit when it comes to helping donkeys. Marina came to Bonaire from Holland in 1990, seeing that there was a big donkey problem and no one addressing it, she dove in and went to work.

After negotiating with the government, Marina secured land near the airport and in 1993 Donkey Sanctuary Bonaire was founded as a nonprofit organization. After 9/11, airport security rules changed and Marina lost her sanctuary and had to relocate and essentially start over again at her current location. Marina, along with her husband Ed Koopman, live on the sanctuary and spend countless sleepless mights nursing orphaned foals and responding to emergency donkey related traffic accidents.

On my return visit to Bonaire while researching and photographing this book, I once again reached out to the opposition group to get a statement, I was once again ignored. But in searching online, I did find some things from them on social media that shed some light on their views. They do not want to see all of the donkeys removed from the wild. They feel that the donkeys are culturally important to the island and should be preserved. They also feel that it is wrong to separate "families" by removing the females and offspring from the males. For the most part, I agree with them. The "families" part is a stretch and is counter to wild donkey's typical behavior. For all my years in donkey rescue, my breath still catches in my throat when I see a free roaming donkey. It is an awesome sight to behold and I would hate to think of a time when none remained, but management is crucial. Overpopulation leads to overgrazing and habitat destruction, especially when drought conditions persist. Overpopulation also leads to more donkey related traffic accidents and dead and maimed donkeys.

A few years ago, the government's biologist did several reports detailing the destruction of the island's eco system due to donkey overpopulation. Unlike other islands that have many goats and cattle roaming as well, on Bonaire it is the donkeys that are the most obvious. One government plan sent 70 donkeys to Curacao to be fed to the lions at the zoo. Another plan called to send 200 wild jacks to Haiti to be used as beasts of burden. This plan was thwarted by supporters that sent a petition to the government with thousands of signatures.

Some new friends I made at the sanctuary

A jack walking along and crossing a busy road

I think everyone can come out a winner on Bonaire, the donkeys can be kept safe, the population can be reduced through attrition and wild donkeys can still roam free. It all needs to start with controlling the population now. Stop the breeding, keep managing the females on the sanctuary and in time, there will be a manageable donkey population. Due to public pressure, the government has stopped the contract with the sanctuary that allowed for the removal of all females and the castration of some males. 1000 donkeys on a 114 square mile island is excessive and if the plan is not set in motion again, the overpopulation problem will just get worse. There are over 600 donkeys on the sanctuary and 400 free roaming. If allowed to breed unchecked, that 400 can more than double every four years and in less than a decade, Bonaire could see 1000 donkeys outside the sanctuary and 600 inside, that is just not sustainable.

Donkey rescue is expensive, as a guy that cares for around 3000 at any one time, I know first hand what it costs to properly care for donkeys. Therefore places like the Donkey Sanctuary Bonaire are static, whatever they bring in must stay in and must be fed and provided for on a constant basis. Unlike our ranch in Texas where we can grow a certain percentage of our own feed, everything on Bonaire must be brought onto the island on a regular basis. The Sanctuary feeds $6,750 of hay from Venezuela and $4,000 of pelleted feed form Holland every month and as the drought affected their water well they are now on a local water supply that costs an additional $600 per month. The Netherlands spends a great deal of money on various projects on Bonaire. They allocated $497,000 to eradicate the goats from Washington Park. They spent $76,000 to get rid of the wild pigs, $473,000 for plants and small tree management but nothing to help with the donkeys.

I encourage you to visit Bonaire, it has everything you want for an island vacation but is laid back and not over crowded. While you are there, visit the Donkey Sanctuary Bonaire. Pay the admission fee, buy some souvenirs in the gift shop and leave a large donation for the donkeys.For those unable to travel, please visit their website at www.donkeysanctuary.org and donate online.

Slave huts along the south shore, obelisk in the background

Breakfast time in the feed barn

Kite surfing near the salt pans

Scuba lesson at the Divi Flamingo

Wind surfing on the East Coast

Sailboat with Klein Bonaire behind

Come and get it!

Marina, surrounded by her volunteers, and me

Sint. Eustatius (Statia)

Country: Netherlands (Special Municipality)

Capital: Oranjestad

Area: 8 square miles

Human Population: 3,193

Donkey Population: 78

Florida

THE BAHAMAS

NASSAU

HAVANA

CUBA

Cayman Islands

GEORGE TOWN

Guantanamo Bay

HAITI

PORT-AU-PRINCE

DOMINICAN REPUBLIC

SANTO DOMINGO

KINGSTON

British Virgin Islands

SAN JUAN

ROAD TOWN

CHARLOTTE AMALIE

Virgin Islands

PUERTO RICO

Anguilla
THE VALLEY

ANTIGUA & BARBUDA

BASSETERRE

SAINT KITTS & NEVIS

ST. JOHN'S

Montserrat

Guadeloupe
BASSE-TERRE

DOMINICA
ROSEAU

Martinique
FORT-DE-FRANCE

CASTRIES
SAINT LUCIA

BARBADOS

KINGSTOWN

BRIDGETOWN

SAINT VINCENT & THE GRENADINES

GRENADA
ST. GEORGE'S

CARIBBEAN SEA

Aruba

ORANJESTAD

Netherlands Antilles

WILLEMSTAD

PORT-OF-SPAIN

TRINIDAD & TOBAGO

CARACAS

A RICA

PANAMA

PANAMA

COLOMBIA

VENEZUELA

Sint. Eustatius, or as I will refer to it throughout this section Statia, was first seen by Columbus on his second voyage in 1493. I won't use the word "discovered" as I think that credit should go to the Arawaks and Caribs that lived throughout the region first. Columbus named the Island after Saint Eustace, a second century Roman general who apparently saw a crucifix in a stag's antlers and converted to Christianity. Just as a side note, virtually all of the Caribbean indigenous people were rounded up to be enslaved and used in mining and agriculture, many perished from the new diseases that the Europeans brought with them.

Formerly a part of the Netherland Antilles, Statia became a "Special Municipality" of the Netherlands in 2010 and has their own island governing body. Bonaire and Saba are also "Special Municipalities" and are often referred to as the BES Islands. Statia lies in the northern Leeward Islands portion of the West Indies and is southeast of the Virgin Islands.

From the 17th century to the early 19th century, Statia changed hands 22 times. During its hay day, it was under Dutch control and was called the "Golden Rock" for the prosperity of the island. As there were no tariffs on trade goods, Statia became the major trading port for all of the New World. Today, you can still see the ancient warehouses that were made from ship's ballast stones along the beach. Statia is odd in that the new and the old live side by side. I cannot say for sure if this is out of respect or indifference.

One last bit of history before we talk about the donkeys is that Statia was the first country to recognize the United States of America. In November 1776, an American warship arrived in the harbor and fired a 13 gun salute, one for each colony in rebellion against Britain. The governor, Johannes de Graaff, responded with an eleven gun salute, international protocol called for a two less gun salute in recognition of a sovereign flag.

Statia supplied nearly half of all armaments and ammunition for our Revolutionary War efforts. In 1781, General John Vaughan and Admiral George Rodney, of the British Empire, invaded Statia with a large fleet and 3,000 soldiers. After taking everything of value, the Admiral and General hung around the island and counted their wealth and ignored orders to proceed to the US and reinforce Cornwallis. They never showed and Cornwallis was forced to surrender to Washington. Had things played out differently, we may have never gained our independence. Thank you Statia, you are welcome USA.

Statia is 8 square miles and has two large dormant volcanoes. There is very little tourism and many of the island inhabitants work for the government. I can find no record as to when the first donkeys came to Statia but it is assumed they were brought in the early 1600s to work the tobacco and sugarcane plantations as well as haul goods and water from the harbor to the fort on the hill. As farming and transportation became mechanized, the donkeys were put out of a job and left to their own devices.

While on the island, I heard some interesting stories about the donkeys. One was that the donkeys would be loaded with water or dry goods down in the harbor, depending on the load the donkeys knew where to go on their own. It was a steep climb up the hill, but they would make the trip several times per day only needing assistance to load and unload. I met an interesting man named Ismael who was over 80 years old. Ishmael told me that when he was young every member of his family had a donkey to work the land and to ride to school.

It should be noted, as this applies throughout the Caribbean, that relocating donkeys from one island to another or even to the mainland would be potentially devastating to the donkeys. Many of these herds have been on these islands for over 500 years and have built their collective immunity around what is prevalent on their particular island. Moving them to an entirely different eco system could kill them.

The old and the new live side by side on Statia

An infrared look at the palm trees around the Old Gin House

To truly understand Statia, you have to realize that there are literally thousands of goats and sheep freely roaming the island. Along with the sheep and goats, there are hundreds of cattle and even some free roaming pigs. All of these animals have financial value and therefore ownership, the donkeys with no value were the first to fall in the crosshairs of the government. A few years ago, the island government decided to cleanup the free roaming animal problem. They passed a few laws directed at getting people to tag their animals, they also decided to round up the donkeys and place them in a pen. No real thought went into the donkey roundup and the donkeys were left to graze in a very limited space. Many died from malnutrition and others, unable to stand, were taken in by a local foundation. It is important to note that the government is resolute, they want no free roaming donkeys on the island. They have even considered shipping all of the donkeys to the French side of St. Martin to be slaughtered for human consumption.

The foundation that was helping the donkeys had no actual donkey experience and very little funding. They reached out to Peaceful Valley for help and in August of 2015, Amy and I flew down to assess the situation. The poor condition of the donkeys was immediately apparent and we called an emergency conference call of our Board of Trustees to secure immediate funding for feed. Peaceful Valley sent the first shipping container of pellets and compressed hay in early September 2015 and have continued to the present. All feed must originate in Florida and the shipping costs are exorbitant.

Aside from the steady supply of feed, PVDR has sent down 3200' of fencing supplies to build a secure sanctuary for the donkeys. We have also purchased two 1000 gallon water tanks and set up a gravity fed water trough system throughout the property. We still need to build additional shaders and an alley and chute system to better medically treat the donkeys.

One of our greatest challenges that we face on all of the islands is the indifference of the locals toward the donkeys. It is virtually impossible to find anyone willing to work at the sanctuary and there is virtually no interest in volunteering. We have sent PVDR employees down on a number of occasions but in the times between visits the donkeys were not receiving consistent quality care. The problem was bad enough that someone cut the fence on the sanctuary letting all of the donkeys loose once again. It also meant that the males and females were mixed and allowed the jennets to be bred.

During my trip to photograph and interview for this book, Donny Raymond, Peaceful Valley Donkey Rescue's International Operations Director, and I met with the island government. Our Trustees had decided that we could not continue to be involved on the island without the sanctuary operating on par with Peaceful Valley standards. We proposed a two year agreement in which all of the donkeys on the island would become the sole responsibility of the Peaceful Valley Donkey Rescue. We would maintain an ongoing presence on the island by rotating our San Angelo Texas staff in 1-3 month shifts.

During the two year period, the local foundation directors and volunteers would have the opportunity to learn from our donkey experts in all aspects of donkey care including medical treatments, hoof trimming and training. We also hope to help them build a fundraising program that will make Statia's donkeys more self sustaining and less reliant on Peaceful Valley.

One thing that struck me about this project is that no one was interacting with the donkeys. They just existed on the sanctuary. I have instructed my staff that they are to spend a minimum of one hour per day interacting with the donkeys and gaining their trust. In the short term, this will make their care and medical treatments easier and safer and in the long term it will help to endear them to the tourists and locals. We intend to do a lot of community outreach by hosting open houses, entering parades and bringing donkeys to local events.

Me, Donny Raymond and Ryan Nealey

Peaceful Valley
Donkey Rescue
International

Sint Eustatius

DONKEY
SANCTUARY

Report Concerns +1 325-234-5169

There is one donkey that we are leaving loose at the request of a local school. This older gelding is very docile and has been adopted by an elementary school that sits outside of town. Donny and I spent several hours looking for him so that we could record his tag number. We searched all of his known haunts and we drove all of the bumpy backroads. We finally gave up and headed to town for lunch just to find the donkey in front of the airport.

While I was on the island there were 32 donkeys on the sanctuary, 33 that had been recaptured and placed in the government's pen and 9 remained loose. As this book goes to print, all of the donkeys have been recaptured and placed on the sanctuary. The males and females are separated once again. The government had ear tags placed in many of the donkey's ears, but they are the large cattle type that have done some damage especially to the young ones. We will be replacing these will small, round, colored tags that have a RFID chip in them, allowing us to identify each donkey individually. At one point, prior to PVDR's involvement, the World Vets came and castrated several of the jacks. We are currently in the process of determining how many whole jacks remain and setting up a castration day with the local veterinarian.

Statia continues to be one of our more expensive projects, especially when viewed on a cost per donkey basis. Our monthly feed cost is $3,600 which will increase as the babies grow and the new foals are born. We are renting a small apartment for the staff at a rate of $750 per month, and every staff change costs $1,400 in travel related expenses. We are also looking to have a truck purchased and shipped to Statia. You can support Statia and our many other donkey projects by visiting our website www.donkeyrescue.org

Statia is a great island to visit. You must first fly into the Dutch side of Sint. Maarten and catch a smaller propeller plane onto Statia. I highly recommend staying at the Old Gin House operated by our friends Sybold and Marlies ten Hoopen. The rooms are very nice and the food is incredible. It sits right on the water and has a great atmosphere. Like most Caribbean islands, everyone speaks several languages, but English is the most common one used. Statia uses the American dollar which is also convenient.

An infrared picture of the Old Gin House

Goats and sheep grazing the local cemetary

Some of the more inquisitive jennets at the sanctuary

Ryan being trained to be our first 30 day full time employee on Statia

Using the government's equipment to return the donkeys to the sanctuary

Nevis

Country: Federation of St. Kitts and Nevis

Capital: Charlestown

Area: 36 square miles

Human Population: 11,108

Donkey Population: 2,000–3,000

Florida

NASSAU

THE BAHAMAS

HAVANA

CUBA

Cayman Islands

GEORGE TOWN

Guantanamo Bay

HAITI

PORT-AU-PRINCE

KINGSTON

SANTO DOMINGO

DOMINICAN REPUBLIC

SAN JUAN

PUERTO RICO

British Virgin Islands

ROAD TOWN

CHARLOTTE AMALIE

Virgin Islands

Anguilla
THE VALLEY

BASSETERRE

SAINT KITTS & NEVIS

ST. JOHN'S

ANTIGUA & BARBUDA

Montserrat

Guadeloupe
BASSE-TERRE

DOMINICA
ROSEAU

Martinique
FORT-DE-FRANCE

CASTRIES
SAINT LUCIA

BARBADO

KINGSTOWN

BRIDGETOWN

SAINT VINCENT &
THE GRENADINES

GRENADA
ST. GEORGE'S

C A R I B B E A N   S E A

Aruba

ORANJESTAD

Netherlands
Antilles

WILLEMSTAD

PORT-OF-SPAIN

TRINIDAD
TOBAGO

CARACAS

A RICA

PANAMA

PANAMA

COLOMBIA

V E N E Z U E L A

In June of 2015 I was approached by a lady from the island of Nevis named Jane Ebbitt. Jane operates the C.A.R.E. Nevis dog rescue (Centre for Animal Rehabilitation and Education) and was attending the Caribbean Animal Welfare Conference along with myself and Peaceful Valley's senior staff that was being held in Costa Rica. Jane had told me about the thousands of Nevis donkeys and the fact that no one was doing anything to help them.

In planning this book, I wanted three different islands with completely different problems. Statia was of course my first thought as we were already there actively saving donkeys. Statia's is a small problem because there are less than 100 donkeys. Bonaire was chosen because you had the Sanctuary and a population control solution but you also had the opposition. There are many donkeys on the sanctuary and almost as many off the sanctuary.

Here on Nevis you have nothing.

Nevis is pretty small, even by Caribbean Island standards. At only 36 square miles you cannot help but see donkeys everywhere. There is a road that rings the island and we drove it twice, thankfully Jane and her husband Patrick were kind enough to drive me so that I didn't have to attempt to drive on the left hand side of the road. Nevis was named for the clouds circling the central volcano. Early spaniards named the island "Nuestra Señora de las Nieves" or "Our Lady of the Snows" which had to do with a miracle snow storm in the mountains above Rome, the clouds apparently reminded them of snow. The island was also known as the Queen of the Caribees for the wealth that the sugar cane brought to the British.

St. Kitts and Nevis are a "commonwealth realm" with Queen Elizabeth II as the official head of state. She is represented by a Governor General , who acts on the advice of the Prime Minister and Cabinet. This system of government is the same as the United Kingdom, Canada and many former British Empire Colonies, including many islands in the Caribbean.

Between 1675 and 1730, Nevis was the headquarters for the African slave trade. 6,000 to 7,000 slaves passed though the island. The first African slaves in Louisiana came by way of Nevis. When slavery was abolished in the British Empire, the slave owners received compensation from the British government for their loss of property, the slaves received nothing. Nevis was plagued by famine during this time and hundreds of former slaves died. Sugar cane production ended in 1706 due to a French invasion but the donkeys were still employed on the many small plots of land used by slaves to grow their own food.

In 2008, Ross University, a for-profit Veterinary college owned by Devry, was accused by PETA of using dogs, sheep and Nevis donkeys in cruel and unnecessary surgeries. I could not find anything to prove this happened or that their practices were any different from what is done in most Veterinary schools in the United States. I did find a Ross University related message board where many of the students disputed PETA's claims.

One indicator of a healthy donkey population is whether or not the jennets are bred and still have last year's foal at their side. Nearly every jennet I photographed had at least last year's foal and many had the previous year's as well, they were all extremely pregnant. The donkeys are in overall good health and the rangeland that they were grazing was in good shape. We found donkeys on the beach, in the parks, in the cemeteries, along the roads, it was mind blowing. The island is also home to 24,000 green vervet monkeys. This is an African breed and is not indigenous to the area. The government is currently considering ways to control the monkey population. I saw cattle, goats and sheep on Nevis but not close to the number or density that I found on Statia. As on Bonaire, the donkeys were the most prominent free grazing animal on the island. It is interesting to note that the two species that originated in Africa thrive so well in the Caribbean. It is very similar to the pythons in the Florida Everglades.

Pregnant jennet with last year's foal grazing in a church parking lot

A small herd of donkeys grazing along a busy road

The thing that struck me while I was on Nevis was the fact that with all of these free roaming donkeys there wasn't a single advocate, no one and I mean No One is looking out for them. In one instance I found a jennet that was extremely pregnant and was lying on a road with what appeared to be a broken hip. We could only assume that she was hit by a car but with the condition of the road forcing you to drive slowly it seemed that it might have been intentional. This would fall in line with rumors I heard while on Statia that some people on Nevis drive around late at night and shoot the donkeys from the back of pickup trucks for fun.

Before I arrived on the island I reached out to one of the island veterinarians. This particular veterinarian had attended a conference in Miami that related to overpopulation problems in the Caribbean. I never heard back from her but while I was on the island I learned that the local veterinarians refuse to work on the donkeys no matter what the situation is. I was also told that there is only one person who will shoot a donkey to relieve its misery and he was currently off island. We contacted the police but four hours later, the donkey was still alive and suffering.

In another instance, Jane received a call about a donkey with something stuck on its front hoof. Patrick and I tracked it down just to discover that her foal was also entangled in something as well. There was nothing available to catch them and remove whatever it was. This was extremely frustrating because if we were in the United States both of these cases could have been resolved easily. On Nevis they seemed overwhelming.

Tetanus is a terrible bacteria that lives in the soil and thrives in warm wet conditions. Donkeys, or other animals, that get entangled in wire or other objects are at risk of coming down with this condition. Tetanus causes muscle spasms and if left untreated, can be so severe that it breaks bones, this is a terrible way to die and easily avoidable with an inexpensive injection.

Jane Ebbitt interacting with one of the donkeys we found chained with water buckets

What Nevis needs is a small sanctuary and donkey knowledgeable people with a truck and trailer. This would give the locals someone to call to respond to donkey related emergencies. The sanctuary could be small, less than four acres. One of those acres could be set up as a traditional sanctuary where donkeys with health issues could live and be gentled. Educational programs could be established and tourists could visit and help support the sanctuary financially. The remaining acreage would be fenced but left open for the majority of the time. Food and water would be made available and the donkeys could come and go as they wanted. Over time, the donkeys would become comfortable with the area and on scheduled days, they could be locked up, sorted, tagged and castrated.

There really is no way to solve the Nevis problem, especially in the short term. There are other birth control methods that are available but they require injections every few years and to be truly effective, the jennets would need to be easily identifiable. A donkey's gestation period is right at 12 months and can get pregnant almost immediately after giving birth. Young females can reproduce at around three years. Without a way to capture, age and catalog the Nevis donkeys there is no way to tell how long they live on the island but it is clear that the overpopulation is only going to get worse.

Donkey rescue is in my blood, it is how I think, it is my primary motivation. Seeing the donkeys on Nevis was an eye opening experience. In the United States, we get involved in projects all across the country, some involving one donkey some involving several hundred, but none of these projects ever seem daunting. Perhaps it is because I am from there, I know the capabilities of my staff, I have confidence in the resources we can bring in and I have faith in my donors to support our efforts. Here on Nevis, I was without a single one of those things. I felt totally over matched. If I were 20 years younger, I could step up and put together a rescue plan that would have a positive impact on the donkey's of Nevis, but alas, I am not 20 years younger. The donkeys of Nevis need a champion, much like the dogs of Nevis have Jane and Patrick Ebbitt.

China consumes 4,000,000 donkeys every year. They eat the meat but it is the hides that they want the most. The hide is boiled down into a gelatin. This gelatin is thought to have healing powers and according to Mr. Google; "It is used for a variety of conditions including bleeding, dizziness, insomnia and a dry cough". At the current rate of slaughter, China's donkey population, once one of the world's largest will cease to exist. Many African countries have either allowed their herds to be decimated or passed laws preventing the export of donkey hides. With demand so high, it is just a matter of time before someone figures out that Caribbean donkeys, like those on Nevis, would make an easy profit on the Chinese market. Especially since there would be no one there to raise a voice in support of them.

On a lighter note, Nevis was a fantastic place to visit. My flight once again originated on Sint. Maarten and took me through St. Kitts before landing on Nevis. The local currency is the Eastern Caribbean dollar, but fear not, every place I visited took US dollars as well. As I said before, they drive on the wrong side of the road, but there are plenty of taxis to take you around to all of the sights. The Oualie Beach Resort is a short drive from the airport. The rooms are in small bungalows scattered around the property. My room was one of four in one of the bungalows. The restaurant was excellent and on Tuesday nights they have live music.

A white woman with dreadlocks sang "I don't want to wait in vain for your love" by Bob Marley, that did it for me. I was already missing Amy something fierce. It was weird being in all of these exotic places without her, so I retired to my room and gave her a call.

I hope you enjoyed this book and have a better understanding of the Donkeys of the Caribbean. Solutions are possible but just like every place else they require money, hard work and someone willing to make the effort. I kept the narration short and to the point as I think the pictures tell the real story. They say a picture is worth a thousand words, so this book is kind of like reading War and Peace.

Y'all be good.

Enjoying the shade and paying his respect

Jennet with broken hip

Two jacks hanging out on the Atlantic Coast

Special thanks to:

Lori Larkin
Horizons Travel Agency
1115 S Abe St
San Angelo, TX 76903
Phone: 325-658-2436

Sybolt and Marlies ten Hoopen
Old Gin House
Inn and Restaurant
Oranjebaai 1, Oranjestad,
Caribbean Netherlands
Phone: 678-534-7125
www.oldginhouse.com
info@oldginhouse.com

Jane and Patrick Ebbitt
C.A.R.E. Nevis
PO Box 298
Charlestown, Nevis
SKN West Indies
www.carenevis.org
info@carenevis.org

Marina Melis
Donkey Sanctuary Bonaire
PO Box 331
Bonaire
+599 95 607 607
www.donkeysanctuary.org
info@donkeysanctuary.org

Amy Meyers
For taking care of da Bean while I was away.

About… well, me

I am the Executive Director of the Peaceful Valley Donkey Rescue. My professional background was in the construction field with a license in both general and electrical contracting. I retired from construction more than a decade ago to concentrate on improving the Plight of the American Donkey.

I have written several books, including the popular series; Talking With Donkeys 1-4. Peaceful Valley and I have been featured both nationally and internationally in television, documentaries, radio and nearly every major market newspaper. Me and Bonney, the oldest of my BurroCollies, were featured by National Geographic. Aside from my rescue duties, I travel the country lecturing to universities and speaking publicly on promoting the welfare of the American Donkey.

My Gear

Canon 5DSr with
28-300mm 1:3.5-5.6

Canon 5D Mark III with
16-35mm 1:2.6 or
150-600mm 1:5-6.3

Canon 7D Mark II with
24-105mm 1:4
720nm infrared filter placed
on sensor

Monfrotto 190Go!
Travel tripod

Peaceful Valley's Mission is to provide a safe and loving environment to all donkeys that have been abused, neglected or abandoned and wild burros under threat of destruction.

Peaceful Valley strives to provide solutions to the many problems that plague these wonderful creatures by providing ethical stewardship over the funds that are necessary to fulfill this goal.

Peaceful Valley, with its nationwide network of Ranch Facilities and Satellite Adoption Centers, is the country's leader in Rescue, Sanctuary, Adoption and Education.

Together, we can improve the Plight of the American Donkey.

Our Humble Beginning...

Mark and Amy Meyers started the Peaceful Valley Donkey Rescue as a backyard hobby over a decade ago. After purchasing their first donkey Izzy as a pet, the Meyers' began to notice other donkeys in their community that were in various stages of abuse and neglect. Not knowing exactly what to do, Amy began buying up these donkeys and Mark spent his evenings talking to the donkeys and fixing their various ailments. It was after the 25th donkey came into the Meyers' home that they decided to open an actual Rescue so that they would be able to find safe, loving homes for their donkeys.

This simple gesture of love has turned into the largest rescue of its kind. The Meyers' still stay involved in the day to day operations of the Rescue but they also manage a large staff that ensure the well being of the over 3,000 donkeys under their direct care.

Under the Meyers' direction, Peaceful Valley has grown to the largest rescue of its kind with facilities all across the United States and now the Caribbean.